# How women Can Succeed in the Workplace

## (Despite Having "Female Brains")

Based on the Powerful, Practical and Entertaining Talk
Given at Colleges, Conferences and Companies
Across the Country

**by Valerie Alexander**

Author Photo by Samantha Ronceros

Cover Design by Valerie Alexander

Cover Layout by Joshua Barragan

Internal Page Layout by Ramesh Kumar Pitchai

ISBN-13:978-1505677522

ISBN-10:1505677521

*Special thanks to my amazing husband, Rick Alexander, the most evolved man I know, for his support, smarts, humor and proofreading skills, and for letting me use him as an example every now and then.*

This book is dedicated to all of the women who have seen this talk live and encouraged me to put it in writing, and to all those who will use the content in these pages to rise through the ranks in their respective fields, take their rightful places at the table, and change the world for the better – for all of us.

# TABLE OF CONTENTS

# ABOUT "FEMALE BRAINS"

In the Fall of 2011, I was invited to give a talk at the Los Angeles Film School about what it takes to be a successful woman in Hollywood. Having just discovered two fascinating areas of academic study – the gendered brain and the evolution of the brain – I decided that what would be of most interest to me, and thus what I could probably make most fascinating for the audience, was how the differences between male and female brains came into being, and how those differences affect female success in the entertainment industry.

**"Why doesn't anyone ever talk about this topic in this way?"**

The talk was very well received; so much so that it's been a repeat event there and almost everywhere it's been delivered. And the most frequent comment I hear after giving it is, "Why doesn't anyone ever talk about this topic in this way?" In other words, why do we force ourselves to do all sorts of interpretive gymnastics to NOT say what is true? Men's brains and women's brains are different, and those differences are reflected in how we behave and are perceived in the workplace.

If that sentence has already made your blood boil, then you're not going to enjoy the rest of this book. Believe me, in the three years that I've been giving this talk – at colleges, film schools, women's networking groups, corporations and conferences – I have met with more than my share of naysayers, who want to vehemently deny that there are any inherent differences in our brains.

On this topic, however, the jury is no longer out. Between behavioral reviews, biological studies, functional MRIs, psychiatric, psychological and evolutionary findings and a whole host of other evidence, we now know that there are fundamental differences between the gendered brains. Just because the science doesn't conform with someone's pre-conceived worldview, it doesn't mean the science is wrong.

Having researched this topic at length, both through academic study and empirical observation as a woman who has been successful in a number of male-dominated fields, let me assure you that I have seen in real life all of the things that the science of brain evolution asserts.

I have been a corporate securities lawyer, an investment banker in the tech sector, and the Vice President of Business Development at two Internet start-ups. Following those careers, I moved to Hollywood and now work as a screenwriter and a film director, in addition to being an author, speaker and life coach.

In the past three years, I have shared the information contained in these pages with a wide array of audiences and been asked to write it as a book on a number of occasions, but I never felt that doing so was really necessary. That changed in August of 2014, when this talk was one of the workshops at the Community Development Foundation's Reality Check Conference, an annual event in Los Angeles for women and girls living in public housing who are enrolled or about to enroll in college.

One of the attendees, a female firefighter, told me that the information in my talk kept her from quitting her job, which she was planning to do the next day. She shared with me what a struggle it is for women in the LAFD, and said she wished she could remember every word from our session so that she could get other women to understand it. She wanted them to realize, as she had during the workshop, which areas of conflict are not their fault, but simply the inherent nature of men and women in the workplace. According to her, this information would keep others from giving up and leaving the field.

Shortly after that, the Executive Director of the CDF came to find me, to tell me all the feedback she'd been hearing about my session, and asked if I had a written version of the workshop that she could share with those who weren't in attendance. Then she said, "I just wish what you talked about could have reached so many more people."

That's when I decided to put it all in writing.

What follows is an amalgamation of the various versions of this lecture that I give for college and graduate students, lawyers and finance professionals, women in the entertainment industry and others.

Periodically throughout the text below, I will share what would be on an accompanying slide or video, and the tone of this entire text is conversational, as if I'm speaking in the room. The talk itself is more dynamic than just the words on these pages, including slides, video and audience participation, so if you'd like to bring it to your campus, company, conference or organization, please reach me at info@SpeakHappiness. com. Also, if you'd like to get on my mailing list, please sign up at http://www.speakhappiness.com/hello/.

One more note before we get started – I do not support and will never engage in male-bashing. I find it insulting and abhorrent to the discussion to talk about *qualitative* differences between men and women, or male brains and female brains. What is the point? Our brains are different. This has been scientifically proven. All the ramifications of those differences are yet to be explored or understood.

I believe that educated adults are able to reasonably investigate this topic and enhance our understanding of it without any need to say that one form of natural, instinctive, evolved behavior is any better or worse than another. Let's look at the facts and figure out how to use them to achieve the optimal outcome – for all of us.

*"Ignorance more frequently begets confidence than does knowledge: it is those who know little, not those who know much, who so positively assert that this or that problem will never be solved by science."*

– Charles Darwin, *The Descent of Man*

# BREEDING FOR INSTINCT

My dog is a German Shepherd. My previous dog was a German Shepherd. I guess I'm in a German Shepherd rut. Either that, or I just really like smart dogs. Life is much easier when your dog is intelligent, trainable and eager to engage.

But I can't deny that German Shepherds have a built-in set of instincts as well. In many ways, they come pre-programmed.

In fact, when I say I have a German Shepherd, what facts can you already assume about my dog? What do you think she's good at just by hearing those two words: German Shepherd?

She's protective? Smart? Well suited to law enforcement and military work? Loyal? Dedicated?

In the years I've given this talk, I've heard dozens of great guesses, but almost never has anyone said the obvious answer on the first try.

It's in the name. German *Shepherd*.

While we rarely think of this breed in this way, my dog is actually quite good at herding. She is, after all, a shepherd.

At this point in the talk, I show a slide of my dog herding sheep. I explain that this picture was taken exactly five minutes after the first time she saw a sheep in her life, and exactly 30 seconds after she was placed in a pen with them.

She wasn't hunting or attacking, she was herding.

## Selecting for certain traits programs some mammals to behave a certain way instinctively

I then show a slide of a Golden Retriever and ask what this dog might be good at. Everyone gets that on the first try – retrieving.

I bring this up because it proves that selecting for certain traits programs some mammals to behave a certain way instinctively. After roughly 8,000 years of breeding dogs to work for and with us, we have isolated different traits and instilled them in different breeds.

German Shepherds have been around since 1899, not even 120 years, and they were never bred to herd sheep. They were bred for working as protectors and soldiers, but they were selectively bred from the descendants of herding dogs, so even though my dog is more than 30 generations removed from the original herders that she came from, she still has all of the herding instincts. Instincts that were bred into her for thousands of years. Instincts that your average Golden Retriever does not have.

So, how does all of this relate to what we're talking about in this book?

Dogs have had about 8,000 years of selective breeding for certain instincts.

Humans have had a lot more time than that.

# THE EVOLUTION OF THE GENDERED BRAIN

If you are reading this book, you are a homo sapiens. Contrary to popular use, you are not a homo sapien. There is no such thing as a sapien. The word *sapiens* in an adjective, meaning wise, or knowledgeable, modifying the word homo, meaning human. A wise human is a homo sapiens.

There is a great deal of debate as to how long homo sapiens have been around, anywhere from 400,000 to 90,000 years, depending on which archaeologist or evolutionary biologist you ask, but we humans are all, definitely, homo sapiens. We walk upright and are no longer covered with hair, although some are more hirsute than others.

There were a whole slew of homo-this-or-thats before us, but we are understood to be the last remaining descendants of the homo hominids, who showed up on the scene and started doing all kinds of cool things, like using tools, building fires and developing language, about 2.3 million years ago, give or take a quarter million years.

The other thing our distant relatives, the homo hominids, did was to start living as groups. They formed hunting packs and tribes that weren't strictly based on familial relation, which meant that there was now a new survival instinct to consider – not just the survival of yourself and your offspring, but also the survival of the pack.

Pretty soon they realized that if a pack has ten men and ten women, and the ten women go off to hunt a wooly mammoth or fight off invaders, and only two women come back, the pack doesn't survive. But if ten men go off to hunt or fight a war, and only two come back, the pack is just fine.

Why? Because ten men and two women cannot reproduce quickly enough to repopulate the pack, whereas ten women and two men can. Survival of the group depended not only on reproduction, but on the offspring surviving until they could reproduce, and since childbirth was such a high-risk activity, and infant survival was iffy at best, female bodies were more biologically valuable to the tribe. Thus, female bodies had to be kept away from activities that were likely to result in a high probability of instant death.

So the tribes specialized by gender. The men were responsible for killing the meat and protecting the cave, and the women were responsible for *absolutely everything else!*

They cooked the food, prepared the skins, made the clothing, made tools, planted seeds, hunted small animals, foraged, fished, raised the children, cared for the sick, kept the fire burning, and so on. No matter what it was, if it didn't have a high probability of instant death, the women did it.

Sadly, the female side of pre-history was left out of evolutionary biology for the better part of a century. Charles Darwin was so committed to proving that the evolution of mankind created a superior male that the entire field dismissed any notion of a female as anything other than weak and dependent, simply because she did not engage in physically aggressive activities.

Darwin's *Descent of Man* was published in 1871, and following that, Darwin's adherents continued to buoy his theories of an active male and a sedentary female. The most prominent names in the field, including Carl

Vogt, George Romanes, Paul Topinard, Paul Broca and Gustave Le Bon, men whose work continues to be studied today, all promoted theories of evolution that favored male superiority. In fact, the underlying thread to their work was that since men had to protect women to ensure reproduction, women were anathema to the success of evolution, since the weaker ones weren't being pruned from the pack.

It wasn't until 1967 that someone finally challenged the notion that women were useless, except in their role as brood mares. What happened in 1967?

A woman entered the field.

In her dissertation at U.C. Berkeley, *Human Locomotion: A Reappraisal of the Functional and Anatomical Evidence*, Adrienne Zihlman took on the entire horde of men who preceded her, arguing that women were as essential to the survival of the pack and the species as men.

This was a major leap forward in the field of evolutionary biology, but it was not enough to overcome the prejudice in the 1970s and '80s – the height of the women's rights movement – against any theory that the male brain and the female brain were different, because those theories were misused so badly for so long. Even today, science and sociology still need to catch up with the idea that different does not mean "better" or "worse."

> We can't ignore two million years of gender specialization when considering how our brains evolved

So my position has always been that we can't ignore two million years of gender specialization when considering how our brains evolved. We know that brain activity and instinct are hereditary traits, as we can see in almost every study of siblings who were separated at birth, or children who are raised by someone other than their biological parents.

Yes, nurture plays a part, but overwhelmingly, nature is dominant, whether we're talking about intelligence or musical talent or even as small a quirk as religious devotion, as shown in the "Switched at Birth" episode of the radio program, *This American Life*. In that story, the biological daughter of a fire-and-brimstone preacher who was raised by a non-religious family still found her way not only to devout Biblical studies, but even to a desire to preach. Where did that come from, if not the brain she was born with?

In my own life, I had a friend who found her biological family while we were in school together, and I accompanied her when she met them for the first time – her mother and seven siblings. Within moments, it was clear that they all had essentially the same brain. Five of the seven kids were working in the same field, which was my friend's field of study at the time, and one of them even told *the same joke* that my friend had been telling for years. These aren't accidents.

My thoughts on this whole issue took a giant leap forward last year, after having given this talk for well over a year, when I had the privilege of watching Dan Gilbert's 2004 Ted Talk on the Science of Happiness.

In it, Gilbert reveals that our brains underwent a massive evolutionary change over the period from 2 million years ago to 400,000 years ago, during which time they tripled in size. But they didn't just blow up like balloons. Rather, they started adding compartments for different functions, and specifically, they added the region known as the prefrontal cortex. This is the part of the brain that controls decision-making, social interaction and emotional response.

What hit me hardest about that fact is the unmistakable coincidence of the timing. We formed a prefrontal cortex *after* we started living in groups. In other words, and pay attention to this, because it is mighty profound: the portion of our brains that controls decision-making, social interaction and emotional response *didn't exist until after we had already specialized by gender!*

How can anyone continue to deny that the male brain and the female brain evolved differently when, as the brain was tripling in size, the men who were most likely to pass their genes on to the next generation were the ones who excelled at hunting and combat and the women who were most likely to pass their genes on to the next generation were the ones who excelled at keeping their offspring alive, which generally involved all non-aggressive survival activity?

What this means is that the male brain developed and honed those traits that were most valuable to their endeavors – namely, quick decision-making, aggression, competitiveness and the ability to be completely at rest when not called upon.

Yes, that last one is a survival trait. If you are sitting behind a rock for two days waiting for a saber-toothed tiger to wander by, or you are stuck in a foxhole for a week in a standoff with enemy combatants, you will be far more successful if you can quiet your brain, wait patiently, and be ready to spring into action at a moment's notice.

Of course, in our modern times, we don't always see it that way.

And by "we," I mean women.

If a man and a woman are sitting quietly in a room and nothing is happening, what is the worst thing she can turn to him and ask?

*"What are you thinking?"*

It's the question that strikes fear in the hearts of even the manliest of men because the answer is often, honestly, "...Um, nothing."

*And there's nothing wrong with that!* Two million years of selective breeding have gotten us to this point, where a man can sit and be thinking <u>nothing</u>. Women shouldn't fault them for that. It means that if we ever need them to go kill a mastodon on short notice, they'll be ready.

Women's brains, on the other hand, evolved to ensure success at all tasks other than mortal combat, often simultaneously. We multitask, we express emotions, we make decisions collectively, we work cooperatively, favoring inclusion over competition, and we'd rather take the time to get to the right answer than make a decision that could be wrong.

Again, it's important to remember that neither of these trait profiles are *better* or *worse*. They were both equally valuable to the survival of the individual, the pack and ultimately, the species.

The conflict between them only arose when more complex societies were formed, gender roles became less clearly delineated, and the whole system tended to favor and reward some inherent traits over others.

# THE EVOLUTION OF COMPLEX STRUCTURES

Men left the caves and women stayed home. Primarily, the men left to engage in hunting and warfare, but eventually they came into contact with others for purposes other than violent conflict, such as trade and commerce. Since men were the ones who were out engaging, and they were only engaging with other men, they were the ones who built the systems of trade and commerce, based on how men behave.

As more and more complex societies emerged, more and more systems were being built. Not just trade and commerce, but now religious systems, military, political – all designed by men.

And I ask you – if you were building a system from the ground up, would it not reflect the traits that *you* already excel at and naturally possess? And if you ran that system for several millennia, wouldn't it be designed to reward those traits, above all others?

We see evidence of this in almost every workplace. The traits that are inherently male, that ensured success at hunting meat and protecting the cave, are the ones that are most highly valued – aggression, competition and quick decision-making.

Going back to our two dogs, the German Shepherd and the Golden Retriever, which is more valuable, herding or retrieving? Which traits are better?

Think very hard about your answer.

The most natural response is to ask, "Well, do you have a bunch of sheep that need to be gathered together, or did you just shoot a duck out of the sky and it fell into a lake?"

In other words, asking which is better begs the question of what tasks need to be performed. And I'm here to tell you, that is the completely wrong way to look at it.

All that matters in the matter of which is "better" is **who decides**.

If German Shepherds are running Canine, Inc., then they are in charge of deciding what all dogs are worth to the organization. In that case, what trait will they determine is most important? That's right. **Herding**.

Herding might not be that great for your endeavor, but as long as Shepherds are in charge, herding is the benchmark. And, after enough time has passed, no one will even question whether or not it should be, whether or not that results in the best outcomes.

If ducks are falling out of the sky and the entire business model of Canine, Inc. is based on someone going and

**As long as they are the only ones designing the system, the system will continue to regard their contributions as more valuable**

getting them, Shepherds still have no incentive to reward retrieving over herding. So they will pack the lower ranks with Retrievers, and allow them to do those tasks, and refer to it as grunt work (thus further convincing the Retrievers that their contribution has less value) and the Shepherds will devise ways to make herding seem important. As long as they are the only ones designing the system, the system will continue to regard their contributions as more valuable.

So Retrievers will always be at a disadvantage and will only be able to advance if they can figure out not only how to herd, but how to herd so effectively that they overcome any judgment that everyone else has already made about their herding abilities based on the fact that they are Retrievers, and not Shepherds.

Then, Retrievers have to be careful not to behave too much like Shepherds, lest they be thought less valuable as Retrievers (or simply too pushy). They also have to distance themselves as much as possible from the Retrievers who are even slightly less proficient at herding, otherwise they will all be lumped in together as lesser herders.

For the Retrievers, it's virtually a no-win situation, until they get to a point where they can show what they bring to the table by being able to retrieve, and how valuable that may be, without posing too much of a threat to the Shepherds. Of course, all but the most evolved Shepherds will still have an inherent need to maintain that herding is superior, but over time, as competitors to Canine Inc. put in the effort to discover which yields the best outcome for the organization (herding, retrieving, or a combo of the two), the workplaces will evolve and the strongest will survive.

But we're not here to make judgments about whether or not the traits we value in the workplace should be the traits we value. That ship has sailed. Two million years of evolution have already pounded into us the traits we value.

What we need to do is figure out how to succeed in a system that rewards traits that may go against our natural instincts, and what steps we can take to redesign that system (from within – which means getting in and doing well under the current structure), so that the traits that are valued and rewarded are those that lead to the best outcomes for the entire organization, regardless of whose evolutionary advantage they reflect.

So what do women need to train ourselves to excel at in order to compete in any male-dominated field? The things that come more naturally to men:

1.  Quick Decision-Making

2.  Hierarchical Structures

3.  Speaking the Language of Success

Plus Seven Irrefutable DOs and DON'Ts that will benefit all women who want to succeed in any workplace.

# QUICK DECISION-MAKING

Men make quick, confident decisions, with limited concern over whether they're right or wrong, and this is highly rewarded in almost every workplace, whether on Wall Street, in Hollywood, or on a farm in Iowa.

The male brain excels at lightning-fast risk analysis, and a willingness to move forward with a decision in the face of risk. This is how the tribe ate.

The female brain wants additional information before choosing a path, often seeking advice and consensus from others, and not always able to commit in the presence of uncertainty. This is how the tribe maintained a well-stocked, smooth running, peaceful habitat.

Bosses and clients value hunters over home-makers.

This fact was drilled into me in my first year of practicing law. I had been representing a small fiber-optics company, we'll just call them Network, Inc., when the senior associate for the client quit, and I inherited his role.

Upon taking over the Network, Inc. files, I quickly discovered they were a mess. The previous associate (let's call him "Ron"), had not exactly been diligent about things like stock issuance and board approvals. It took months of working through them before the corporate documentation was in order and the company was ready for another round of financing or an exit event.

Of course, that's not exactly time a law firm can bill for – no client wants to see "clean up prior attorney's mess" on their bill, so a lot of what I was doing was being written off by the partner I worked for, which was bad for both of us.

Still, it had to be done. Then, one day, the partner walked into my office and said, "I just got off the phone with the CEO of Networks, Inc. They want a different associate. They don't like you. They miss Ron."

To which I replied, "But Ron gave them *horrible* legal service."

And he said, "When they called Ron, he gave them answers and when they call you, you say, 'I'll look into that and call you back.' They don't like that."

"But Ron was WRONG half the time," I exclaimed.

"They don't care. When clients call, they want an answer. Give them one."

And with that, he turned and left.

I sat there, all of 26 years old, mystified that anyone would just want an answer, right or wrong. It wasn't until years later, when I joined an Internet start-up as an executive and was thus on the client side, that I understood what was really going on.

## "When clients call, they want an answer. Give them one."

On the client side, the CEO asks a VP a question, like: "Hey, can we issue stock as Christmas bonuses?" The VP doesn't know, so goes and asks someone in the HR department. HR doesn't know, so asks someone in the finance department. Finance determines that no one really knows, so they'd better ask the company's lawyer.

Now, this is not a cheap call. At my hourly billing rate, a brief call like that was probably going to cost them around a hundred dollars and they knew it, so by the time they decided to call the lawyer, a lot of people really wanted the answer, and were willing to pay for it.

So Finance calls me to ask the question, and, being a diligent attorney, I say, "I don't know. Let me look into that and get back to you." Which I always did, and always within 24 hours, which I thought was pretty good.

But on their side, here's what that looks like:

1. Finance now has to go tell HR, "The lawyer doesn't know. She'll get back to me."

2. HR has to go tell the VP, "The lawyer doesn't know. She'll get back to Finance."

3. The VP has to go tell the CEO, "The lawyer doesn't know. She'll get back to someone."

And now everyone has disappointed the person they report to directly, and they still have to wait to see what my answer is, and maybe that will disappoint all over again.

After I was told to just give them an answer, things went a little differently. Now when the client called, I did a little risk analysis. I thought, "Can they issue stock as Christmas bonuses? Well, it's October, so there's very little risk if I give them the wrong answer and chances are they want to hear, "Yes." So I replied, "Sure." And

Finance said, "Thanks!" and they went back to HR and said, "The answer's 'Yes'," and HR went to the VP and said, "The answer's 'Yes'," and the VP went to the CEO and said, "The answer's 'Yes'," and I hung up and looked up the answer.

Now I knew this client pretty well by that point, and I was right about 75% of the time, and in the times I was wrong, I would call back and it would sound something like this: "Just to be sure, I looked into it further and you're going to need Board approval to do that, so I wrote up a quick letter to send to Board members and I'll shoot it over to you with instructions."

And guess what? NOBODY CARED THAT I WAS WRONG IN THE FIRST PLACE. In fact, you'll notice that at no point in my second call did I say, "I was wrong." What I said was, "You had a problem, but I solved it for you."

**And there is no one we value more highly in the workplace than problem solvers.**

At this point in the talk, I move to the next topic, but for the purposes of this book, I want to share two more examples: One, a real conversation I had with this same client that required a fast risk analysis, and the second, a hypothetical conversation that might take place on a film set between the Gaffer and the DP.

Following is an actual conversation I had with the CEO of Networks, Inc. where the risk of giving a wrong answer was too high to just wing it.

CEO: "Hi Valerie. Can we include an option for 20,000 shares in a job offer for an engineer?"

[At this point, I have to do a fast, but critical, risk assessment.]

Valerie: "Is this just academic or are you making someone an offer?"

CEO: "He's here. We're negotiating. We were at ten and he wanted 25."

[So giving the wrong answer is very risky, as it would be disastrous if they had to rescind the offer, or if they lost a good candidate whose demand could have been met. I need time, so I buy some.]

Valerie: "Do you want to go that high?"

CEO: "We really want this guy."

[By now, I have their share issuance spreadsheet open, but still don't know how much is left in their approved option plan. More stalling, in the guise of legal advice.]

Valerie: "Just so you're aware, there is not an engineer in the building who has an option for more than 10,000 shares. Your VP of Engineering's option is only for 15."

[Silence on his end. This is a big deal from a business perspective and he needs to think about it. Either that or he's annoyed that I would bring that up. Who's to say? Meanwhile, I'm scrambling to add up all their various Board approvals to see how much is left in the plan. Make a note to myself to have this be an ongoing update in the spreadsheet for the future. Find it ridiculous that the document doesn't already include that. Mind dwells on this.]

CEO: "Are you still there?"

[I realize how long the silence has gone on.]

Valerie: "Sorry, I'm doing a little math. This is going to take a few minutes. Do you want to stay on the line or should I call you back?"

CEO: "I'll wait."

After about five more minutes of me pulling out every Board approved allocation of stock to the option plan, and calculating how much was issued and how much still remained, I added the number from the approval I was holding and that put the total at 22,000 shares available.

Now, it is absolutely in my nature to go ahead and calculate all the rest of them, to tell him exactly how many shares are remaining in the option plan, <u>but that is not the question he asked</u>. That is not a question he needs answered while a candidate hangs out in the next room. That is not a question he wants to pay for another minute of my time to get. My job, at this moment, is simply to answer the question he asked.

Valerie: "You have at least 22,000 shares available."

CEO: "Thanks."

And with that, we got off the phone. I never knew if they hired that engineer or gave him the options or not. After that call, I realized that tracking their option plan was a job that could be handled better (and more cheaply for them) by their Human Resources department, so I trained them how to do it.

Because <u>delegation</u> is also a critical aspect of success which women tend to underutilize, but we'll talk about that when we discuss the concept of hierarchical structures.

Going to an entirely different workplace, but with the same principles at play, imagine you're the Gaffer (the chief electrician) on a film set. The production is using house power, which means that all of the electrical equipment is being plugged into the walls at the location, a mansion in the hills. Your Best Boy (the Gaffer's #1 assistant) just walked away with your circuit tester and the DP (the Director of Photography) comes to you holding a plug and asks, "Can I plug this into the wall?"

*"I don't know,"* is a terrible answer.

*"I can tell you in ten minutes,"* is also a fairly unappealing answer.

Remember, film crews are assembled by department heads calling the people they liked working with on the last film and offering them jobs. Giving weak, unhelpful answers means not getting those calls.

Chances are, the DP is asking the question because the Director needs something that requires that thing being plugged in, and nobody ever wants to fail the Director. Also, the most precious commodity on any film set is time. Wasting someone's is a very bad idea. You'll see how ironic this is in a moment.

The only thing to do is perform a quick risk assessment, and give the answer that makes the most sense in your situation. So you start with a question...

Gaffer: "What do you need to plug in?"

DP: "We're shooting night-for-day and I need a 10K to mimic the sun."

[This requires virtually no additional thought. You reply:]

Gaffer: "And you think that can be plugged into the wall of a house? Are you smoking crack? I'll go order a generator." [See...always be problem solving.]

OR...

Gaffer: "What do you need to plug in?"

DP: "The lead actor needs to charge his cell phone."

Gaffer: "Go ahead."

But it won't be that cut-and-dried. It won't be a 10,000-watt bulb versus a cell phone charger. So the conversation will look more like this:

Gaffer: "What do you need to plug in?"

DP: "A bank of fluorescents."

Here's where the lightning-fast risk analysis comes in. You have to decide if it's better to commit a Type I error (saying, "Yes" if you should have said, "No"), or a Type II error (saying, "No" if you should have said, "Yes"). Really you're just buying time without looking indecisive until you **Perform a quick risk assessment, and give the answer that makes the most sense in your situation** can get to the right answer. And yes, I realize this is the bigger waste of time. Therein lies the irony.

What are the risks of saying, "Sure, plug those lights in" if there isn't enough juice on the circuit to support it?

1. Blowing out all the power for the entire location;

2. Shutting down the production;

3. Burning down the mansion

And what are the risks of saying, "No" if there is enough juice?

1. Wasting ten minutes while you get to the right answer;

2. Annoying the DP slightly. Maybe. Or maybe she'll be grateful that you gave a quick answer and will just go look for a different solution.

So, with authority, you say, "No, the circuit can't support it." (Speaking with authority is critical here, which we'll discuss in greater detail when we get to the Language of Success.)

When the DP walks away, you run around until you find your circuit tester and you check the outlet.

If you were right and the circuit did not have enough juice, then you do nothing. Your job is done.

If you were wrong, and the circuit can fully support a bank of fluorescent lights, you go find the DP and say: "Hey, I moved some things onto different circuits and you can plug the fluorescents into that outlet now."

It will not be held against you that you gave the wrong answer, as long as you get to the right answer as quickly as possible, and giving the wrong answer did not hurt the production.

It will be held against you if you get a reputation as someone who can't think on her feet, is wishy-washy, doesn't answer questions, etc.

Sure, you wasted more time than if you'd just gone and checked the circuit in the first place, but no one knows that and no one cares that you were wrong, because now the DP gets the outcome she wants. This makes you a problem solver – the most highly valued person in any workplace.

Does this feel ludicrous to you? That's because it is. But this is also how almost all workplaces operate. Quick decision-making is one of the most highly valued and rewarded traits. When superiors, clients and co-workers want answers, give them answers, and if you're wrong, fix it later under the guise of having solved a problem.

The person who always replies with "I don't know," or "Let me check," or "I have to look that up," is eventually going to be perceived as unable to be relied on, whereas the one who replies confidently and definitively is admired and invited back, again and again. Keep that in mind and work to make quick decisions and act on them confidently, as if you were hunting a wooly mammoth.

I'll say one more thing on this point, then move on. If you find this next part offensive,

> ## Make quick decisions and act on them confidently, as if you were hunting a wooly mammoth

I don't care. It makes the point, and those who fight it are denying our true nature.

Right now, as a woman, picture a fireman. His hat, his boots, his ax, his truck, his chiseled abs, his bravery. His sooty face and faint whiff of smoke, having just rescued a little girl from a burning schoolhouse. Get a full image.

Now, picture a state fire inspector. His clipboard, his bald spot, his glasses, his slight paunch, his state-owned Ford Taurus. Got that image?

Okay...who is your body telling you to mate with? Who does your instinct tell you has a higher probability of producing offspring that will survive into the next generation?

Be honest.

The reason I bring this up is that one of them puts out fires, and one of them prevents fires from ever happening in the first place. And no matter where you are in society – on a movie set, in a corporation, at a law firm, in Washington – across the board, we place a much higher value on the person who can put out fires than on the one who makes sure fires never happen in the first place. Which is ridiculous. It's better to not have fires! But an absence of fires means those with quick reaction, combat-ready skills aren't recognized or rewarded for their strengths.

Think about every workplace you've ever been in, and reflect on who was most respected and rewarded – the person whose good planning and efficient execution made sure a crisis didn't happen, or the person who handled the crisis?

Who is treated with the greatest reverence, the soldier or the diplomat? To answer, how many monuments around the world have ever been erected honoring the ambassador who averted a war?

It is inherent in the male brain to react well to a crisis. To put out fires. To fight the war. To make quick decisions and solve problems. This is what gets rewarded, *even if he was the one who started the fire or caused the problem in the first place.* This is what wins medals. And promotions. And gets written about in the history books and news reports.

It is inherent in the female brain to assess situations holistically, see the places where a fire might start and prevent it. This is overwhelmingly valuable and almost never recognized. Even other women still value the fireman over the fire inspector. We can't help it. Two million years of evolution and all...

So what women have to do to succeed is continue to spot issues and thwart crises before they happen – after all, this is still beneficial – but when they do happen, we also have to be the first-responders. We have to solve the problem and prevent others from taking credit for solving the problem. We have to be the Retrievers who know how to herd.

# HIERARCHICAL STRUCTURE

There's no "I" in TEAM.

There's also no "B"-"O"-"S"-"S"

In a recent talk by Louann Brizendine, author of *The Female Brain* and *The Male Brain*, she discussed a study of six year-olds from a variety of backgrounds in which a group of six year-old *boys* were allowed to play freely together for an hour. After an hour, they were separated and asked who was in charge, and to rank everyone in the group from the top dog all the way down to least powerful.

Not only could every single boy make that list, but all of their lists were virtually the same. Six months later, when the same boys were put together for the same exercise, they made the same lists. In other words, once the order was established, it was maintained.

That experiment was also conducted with six year-old *girls*. Most of them, after an hour of play, could not form a list at all, and refused to acknowledge that anyone was in charge. The ones who did come up with lists, all had different lists.

What does this tell us?

Within a male system, *instinctively*, hierarchy matters. To survive in the tribe, you have to know who is more powerful than you are

# To survive in the tribe, you have to know who is more powerful than you are and who is less powerful and act accordingly

and who is less powerful and act accordingly. The same goes for being at war, but even more so. A clear chain of command is critical for survival. Men know that, and the corporate world they built reflects that, in no uncertain terms.

Who is in charge matters, as does maintaining your place in the hierarchy, or trying to move up. No one wants to work with the person who says, "That's not my job," when asked to do something, or thinks a task is beneath them, and yet, men generally know better than to do the work that is below their status and women don't. Worse, women are often expected to, and we have to find smart, non-alienating ways to hold our ground and say, "No."

When I was practicing law, I shared a secretary who was an older woman, who never quite understood why I had an office and she had a cubicle. She also worked for a male partner, and doing my work was never that high a priority for her. This was extremely detrimental to me, because I was working 70-90 hours a week on a regular basis and desperately needed someone to handle the secretarial side of the job, which she clearly expected me to.

Since I regularly left the office after midnight (or after 2:00 a.m., or not at all...), I would come in around 9:30 most mornings, and she had to clock in at 8:00 a.m., which meant she had an hour and a half to herself every day. So before I left each night, I would type up a list of things I needed done and leave them on her chair to do in the morning, which she routinely ignored.

One night, I left my time sheets for her. Time sheets are how everyone in a law firm gets paid. We charge by the hour, and unless clients know how many hours we've worked and on what, they don't pay us. Every firm has its own elaborate billing system and my firm was no different. Attorneys kept track of time on specially-designed time sheets, and secretaries entered those hours into the system so that bills could be generated and we could all eat.

So my time sheets were sitting on her chair when she arrived and when I got in, a couple of hours later, she came into my office, holding the time sheets and asked, "Would you like me to show you how to enter these directly into the system?"

Stop and think about that question for a minute. She wanted to show me, the lawyer she worked for, how to do her job.

That woman would eat glass before she asked a male attorney if he wanted to learn how to enter his time sheets into the system.

So I looked at her and I said, "I'm pretty sure our clients don't pay $325 an hour for me to enter time sheets into the system. But if you can find someone I can bill it to, I might consider it." She turned and left in a huff.

This got me to wondering what would possess her to even ask me that question, so I started asking around. That's when I discovered a very sad truth about my workplace.

Every other female attorney in my group entered her own time sheets into the system, and not a single male attorney did. In fact, the men were appalled that I would even ask if they did, and one of them didn't even know that there was some system beyond him filling out a form and giving it to his secretary.

So I started asking the women why, and the answers ranged from, "It's not that hard to figure out," to "It's just easier to do it myself." In other words, I don't want to deal with making my secretary do her job.

And to be clear, back then, there was *no way* it was easier to enter the information into the computer than to write it on a pad of paper. It would have meant exiting whatever document or research you were working on, logging into the billing system, entering the Client and Matter numbers and the time, then logging out and going back to work.

Were these female lawyers really doing this every time they did any work for their clients? No. They were writing it on the pads and transcribing it themselves. How is that the most efficient, productive use of their training, education and skills? How does that benefit the clients and the firm?

Worse, many times they were not billing for things that were too small to be worth the trouble, which over time added up to days or weeks of uncredited hours. If you write off 15 minutes every day, that's more than 60 hours in a year, which is more than a full week of billable time.

This is one of the reasons women don't advance in the workplace: we allow ourselves to do work that is beneath our status – to the detriment of the company! The firm wasn't paying those lawyers to do clerical work, and expected them to know better.

Hierarchy matters. If you are the boss, know you are the boss and act accordingly. This also means that your assistant is not your best girlfriend. You don't come in on Monday and tell her about your drunken hook-up over the weekend.

More importantly, you don't complain to her about your job. Your role is to supervise, guide and praise the good work of those who report to you, and if you're having problems with your superiors or colleagues, take it to them, not the person whose respect and dedication you need to succeed.

In 2010, I taught a legal ethics class at Berkeley Law called, "Representations of Law in Film." Since the majority of law professors have never practiced law, and no one teaches things like how to manage your assistant (a critical part of any lawyer's success), I took an hour out of the syllabus one day to cover that for the students in my class.

I made the point that legal assistants were professionals, just like they were, and needed to be treated with the same respect and tone of voice as any attorney in the firm, but that at the end of the day, if there is a conflict, the lawyer has the final say, without further discussion. Rank has its privileges.

I shared the time sheets story, and one other incident, about a secretary who refused to share a printer with another lawyer and me, meaning we had to walk to the other end of the hall whenever we printed documents, despite a printer sitting directly between our two offices. Without going into the details, I won that one, and I did it by playing the "I'm the lawyer here" card (something men almost never have to do because they are *automatically* treated as superiors in the workplace.)

The male students generally felt this was information they already knew, however, what shocked me was the reaction from the female students. In the discussion, several of them balked at the idea of having the last word "simply because I'm the lawyer and she's the secretary," and one even gave me a negative evaluation at the end of the term, saying, "She told us we had to talk down to our assistants." Of course, that is not at all what I was advocating, but the idea that I was telling them to be in charge, without apology or concession, ran contrary to their instincts.

Again, this is a male/female thing. Not one male student thought I should have backed down from the printer-hogging secretary, and most found the whole thing ludicrous, asking, "Why would she even think she could get away with that?" The female students were instead asking me what alternatives I had tried to come up with. They wanted me to have worked towards a consensus solution, rather than just declare my authority.

What a waste of time! When you are higher than someone on the corporate ladder, you don't have time to make sure they agree with all of your decisions, and it's not your job to do so. In male-designed workplaces, knowing where you are in the pecking order and not relinquishing your spot is how you advance and get rewarded. Manage inclusively, and with respect, but at the end of the day, get your way.

Few workplaces are as hierarchical as a film set. The Director is in charge of everyone (with the potential exception of any A-list actors, who sometimes no one can control). All of the department heads report to the Director, and all of the other crew members report to their respective department heads.

Someday, really look at the credits of a movie. You'll see the Director, the First Assistant Director, the Second Assistant Director and the Second Second Assistant Director. That's the hierarchy in just in one team. Similar rankings occur in every other department – Camera, Wardrobe, Construction, Hair & Make-up, and so on. A film crew is like an army and production is like battle, and no one can afford to have even one soldier break ranks.

**When you are higher than someone on the corporate ladder, you don't have time to make sure they agree with your decisions, and it's not your job to do so**

What happens to women in traditionally male crew positions, however, is that they begin performing the tasks of the people beneath them, which is incredibly detrimental to their careers.

If you're the Second Assistant Cameraperson (the 2$^{nd}$ AC) on a shoot and the DP says, "Hey, we ran out of sandbags, can you hold this C-stand while we shoot?" You say, "No problem," because the DP is your boss, and she might be asking you because there's an $80,000 light on the end of that stand and the DP doesn't trust anyone but you.

But if a random production assistant has been told to do it, and tries to get you to do it instead – no way. If you're the 2$^{nd}$ AC and the DP sees you holding a light stand instead of doing your real job, you will quickly be seen as incompetent, and the next time that DP is hired for a movie and needs to crew up, you won't get a phone call.

Knowing your place is especially critical if you're the Director. As women, we are hard-wired to be collaborative and cooperative. It started around the campfire two million years ago. But when you are the Director, you are not a member of the crew. You are the Captain of a very complex ship and you have to be able to say, "Nope. We're not doing it that way, we're doing it this way." Quickly and unapologetically.

Be open to everyone's input; after all, they are artists and professionals, too, and they might know more than you. But that does not mean you defer to their judgment over your own. You aren't being a bitch, no matter what the grips say, and remember, there's no "Boss" in "Team."

In every workplace, know the exact functions and expectations of your job, and only go outside of those if it is going to advance your career, increase your skills or move you *up* the ladder. Know who you are above and who is above you. Don't be afraid to hold your ground, so long as you do it in a way that is respectful and doesn't harm the organization.

Also, when you hold your ground, don't second-guess yourself. Stand by your own positions. Women way too easily yield our place in the hierarchy, and it is almost impossible to recover, but it's far worse when we claim our spot, then tell *ourselves* that we're wrong for doing so.

Remember the six year-old boys?

Six months later, they all had the same lists.

# THE LANGUAGE OF SUCCESS

One of the traits we inherited from our homo hominid foremothers was a desire for consensus. While the men were out hunting, the women were working as a group to ensure all other tasks of survival were performed. Thus, the women who were most successful were the ones who could behave cooperatively and get along with other women.

Among groups of men, the strongest, loudest and most aggressive is generally put in charge, but among women, there are often no leaders, and the few who are chosen are the ones who excel at group dynamics – inclusiveness, fair play and the ability to be task oriented without alienating anyone.

As a result of this, in group situations, women ask for agreement when asserting their positions. We've all been in a meeting where a woman opened her statement with some variation of, "I'm not sure if everyone would agree with this, but..." and then went on to make her (now severely weakened) point.

Do not discount yourself or what you're about to say with the way you announce the information. Don't open a statement with, "I might be wrong here..."

Really? You might be wrong? Then why are we listening to you? Why would *anyone* listen to you?

Women do that sort of thing constantly, and men almost never do.

> Do not discount yourself or what you're about to say with the way you announce the information

Men state their positions, with authority, and are prepared to defend them from the first breath. A woman is concerned with offending people who disagree with her, or intimidating someone who might also have a valid point.

But in the workplace, confidence and competence are perceived as the same thing. An incompetent employee who behaves with great confidence is often perceived as completely competent, while the skills of a highly competent employee who lacks confidence are often perceived to be lacking.

Your opening salvo doesn't even have to be as blatant as, "I might be wrong," to be damaging. In the first example above, something as innocent as "Does anyone else agree..." eliminates the option of that solution if no one else agrees. What if that's the best answer? Now you've lost the ability to vigorously champion it. Why give permission to be dismissed?

If you want to make a point, try one of these powerful openers:

"Here are my thoughts..."

"The solution we need to consider is..."

"I've done a lot of research on this topic, and I believe..."

Then, don't back down instantly at the first challenge (or second!). If someone disagrees, it's not a personal attack, it's an opportunity to rise to the occasion, and calmly and professionally show why your course of action is the best. Be open to being debated, but not disregarded.

Another thing women do is try to ingratiate ourselves to the listener, rather than simply commanding respect with our presence. We try to show up-front that we're not a threat or we acknowledge our own limitations by denigrating ourselves. Women bond over putting ourselves down. It's perfectly natural and it has to stop.

In an earlier example, I talked about a film set where the DP asked the Gaffer if something could be plugged into a wall outlet and the Gaffer said, "No," then later found out that the answer should have been, "Yes." There are a variety ways for that Gaffer to go back to the DP and change the reply, and in the example, I chose to go with saying, "Here, I solved your problem." This is the best choice.

Sadly, sometimes women choose the self-denigration route instead. You would never hear a man in that situation go up to the DP and say, 'I'm a total idiot, and it turns out you can use that outlet." A woman would. If you would – don't.

A friend of mine, a very competent attorney, filed the wrong document with a court one time, and needed the other side to consent to her changing it. This should have been a non-issue, but when she called the opposing counsel, she opened her voice mail message with, "Hey, I blew it..."

She was shocked when the other lawyer, also a woman, used that against her aggressively, even going so far as to play the "I blew it" message for the judge, and challenging the amendment to the filing. I'm not sure if everyone's behavior would have been any different had she left those three words out of the message, but I am sure that she could have found a less self-sabotaging way to present the information.

We have to remember that when we are competing in a male-designed workplace, we are not sitting around the campfire with our girls. Consensus, cooperation and cohesion are not valued in the same way that competition and assertiveness are.

You are not trying to figure out who will mend the loincloths, who will feed the babies and who will skin the fish, you're trying to be the first one out of the bushes to spear the gazelle so that your family will eat.

Doing that doesn't start with telling everyone in the room, "I'm probably way off base here..."

# SEVEN IRREFUTABLE DOs and DON'Ts FOR WOMEN IN THE WORKPLACE

## 1. Do Make Decisions!

To succeed in any competitive workplace, you must make quick decisions, confidently, and not be apologetic or self-deprecating about changing them if they are wrong.

If you're directing a movie and the costumer asks if you want your actress in the red shirt or the blue one, the thing that will achieve the best possible outcome is to gather together the DP, the makeup artist and the actress and see which will look better in the scene, maybe do a camera test, try different lighting with each color, but nobody making a movie has the time for that, so you look at them both and you say, "Blue."

Then, let everyone else do their jobs, and when you look at the monitor, if the shirt looks like crap, you say, "This looks like crap. Get the red shirt in here."

End of discussion. No apology. That is the way to run a film set. That is the way to get all of your shots and make your day. That is the way to ensure that everyone knows that you know what you're doing, even if you feel like you don't. As one of our former Presidents said, be "The Decider."

In any workplace where you are in charge, the first time you have a decision to make, after everyone else has done their part and it's down to you, don't you dare turn to anyone around you and ask, "What do you think?" You will lose all of your authority, whether it's over a film crew or a Wall Street deal team or your Congressional staff.

Just decide.

## 2. Don't Apologize Unless You've Actually Done Something Wrong!

When you make a decision, if it turns out to be incorrect, fix it without apology. That's what men do. Don't call attention to your error. Reserve apologizing for hurting someone's feelings, not doing your job less than perfectly.

I think the apology gene comes from some overwhelming belief among women that if we are imperfect in the workplace, we are doing something wrong. We are letting someone down. I have struggled to figure out why for a while, and the theory I've come up with is that the system was designed to reward traits we don't inherently possess, so we show up already feeling less than adequate. Then, we are surrounded by the people who the system naturally favors, so they seem to be great at jobs that we feel like failures in, with no regard to our respective performances.

The reality is that in the workplace, men are swimming with the current and we are swimming against the current, and rather than acknowledging that, we simply look at them and think, "Damn, they are much better swimmers than we are."

They aren't! In fact, anyone who has spent all her time swimming against the current is going to be a significantly stronger swimmer, but she still won't get as far as anyone swimming with the current, and she will always feel like she doesn't belong among elite swimmers.

Recently, I introduced a friend who hosts a local radio show to a guest she wanted to interview. I made the introduction through email, copying both women, but it got lost in my friend's incredibly packed inbox for a week.

When she did finally reach out, she opened her email with an apology and an explanation of how busy she was. The potential guest replied with some available dates, and when the host responded, she *again* apologized for taking so long to reach out initially. Coincidentally, she and I had to make arrangements for a separate event and in her email to me, she wrote: "My apologies again for missing your introduction email to Michelle. I don't know how I missed that but I feel awful about it. I'm thrilled to get her on the show. Thank you so much for that intro!!"

At that point, I had to say something, so I replied: "So glad it worked out with Michelle. Now, pretend you have a penis and stop apologizing. Shit happens. You're a busy woman." I also didn't need her to thank me again. She had done that enough, too.

As a woman, be cautious not to apologize unless you've actually committed a wrong; don't over-apologize and don't over-thank. Just do your job to the best of your ability.

And don't open your comments in the meeting with, "I'm sorry..."

That's not the Language of Success.

## 3. Don't be Helpful, be Harmless!

Of all the DOs and DON'Ts on this list, this is the one that meets with the most resistance. It is 100% female nature to be helpful at all times, and it is rarely in your best interest. Just be harmless.

Three main reasons not to be helpful are: (1) it might not be what is wanted by the recipient of your assistance; (2) you might be sacrificing your place in the hierarchy; and (3) you may be drawn into a conflict that you need to stay above to do your job.

A friend of mine works regularly as a production assistant on film sets. It's decent pay and he's good at it, and when he's not booked, he will also pick up days working as a background extra through Central Casting, the big player among extras booking services.

One day, while working background, he and several other extras were gathered on set when the First Assistant Director (the 1st AD, the person in charge of keeping a shoot on schedule) came over to give them instructions for the next take, which would be after the meal break. My friend noticed that about a dozen other extras were in a different part of the set and didn't get the instructions, so he trotted after the 1st AD and said, "Hey, you didn't tell those people." The AD didn't really respond, he just turned and walked away.

So my friend took it upon himself to go tell the extras the after-dinner instructions.

Everybody had dinner, then when they started up again, the Director, the 1st AD, the 2nd AD, the Line Producer (the person in charge of keeping a shoot on budget) and several other crew members started getting very angry when they saw all these people.

Turns out, the dozen extras that my friend decided to go talk to had already been released for the day. When he came over to them, they thought he was part of the crew and they were being told to stay.

This meant that the production had to feed and pay overtime for twelve people who had already been told to leave, that their day was done, all because one person decided to be "helpful." When the extras explained why they were still there, not only did my friend get kicked off the set, but the 1st AD (who was now in a lot of trouble with his bosses) called Central Casting and reported him as a trouble-maker, which got him banned. He lost about $500 a month in income as a result.

If you think it was the 1ˢᵗ AD's fault for just walking away without explaining anything, I have to point something out. On film productions, 1ˢᵗ ADs are generally the busiest people on set. They are managing logistics for every single aspect of the day to keep things moving as close to on schedule as possible, which is nearly impossible. Chances are very good that right when my friend was talking to him, someone else was reporting a crisis in his earpiece and he just turned to go deal with it.

Also, keep in mind that film sets require strict adherence to the hierarchy. No 1ˢᵗ AD in the history of cinema has ever had to explain himself to an extra. My friend was wrong, and he paid the price.

Speaking of hierarchy, another reason not to be helpful is that it might cost you your place in the pecking order, which is virtually impossible to recover from. I can't tell you how many meetings I've been in that end with the men all getting up to leave the room and the women – women of equal stature – picking up trash and dishes. If it's not your job to clean the room, don't clean the room unless *everyone* is doing it.

As an investment banker, I would often be the only woman in a room where high-level negotiations were taking place, and at some point, someone would always mention that we needed a note-taker. I never volunteered. In fact, on more than one occasion, the man in charge would simply turn and say, "Valerie, would you take notes?" and my reply was always, "Why don't we see if someone's secretary is available, so I can participate fully?"

At that point, sometimes one of the junior bankers in the room would offer to do it, which was fine, or even one of the senior bankers, as if proving some point. That was fine, too. I know it probably offended the asker that I refused, but not nearly as much as it offended me that I was the first one asked. I needed to make it clear that even though I may look more like your assistant than the other people in this room, I did not just get sent here from the steno pool. The same person never asked me twice.

When you're the only Golden Retriever in a room full of German Shepherds, and the job of the day is herding, don't offer to retrieve, and don't let them ask you to. If you're herding white sheep, black sheep and rare, valuable pink sheep, and you're on the pink sheep team, and someone points out that they need more herders on the white sheep team, don't you dare open your snout to volunteer. You will lose your spot at the table that you worked so hard to get. Let someone else be helpful.

And the final reason not to be helpful is that it might put you in a situation you'd be better off staying out of. You do not need to referee anyone else's conflicts. Assume everyone is an adult, and let them take care of themselves. If it's your job to manage the people in question, or if your job performance is going to be hurt by their drama, behave according to your role in the hierarchy and don't be any more helpful than that.

Back to my old law firm, there was an assistant in our department who was married to an assistant in another department, and that other assistant had a running conflict with one of our paralegals, which eventually got him fired.

None of the male attorneys in the group were even aware of any of this until the day the feuding assistant was walked out of the building by security, and yet, several of the female attorneys had wasted ridiculous amounts of time speaking to both parties, mediating and just putting themselves in the middle of it.

I was not one of them.

To me, the best course of action is to walk away from crazy.

Don't be helpful, be harmless.

# 4. Do Network and Help Each Other Out!

I didn't realize it until I got married, but women are horrendous at networking. I thought we were okay, and then I saw how my husband and his friends behave and I could not believe what they did, and how badly we were doing it.

My husband is a screenwriter and producer. Whenever one of his friends gets a new job as an executive at a film studio or television network, the first thing that man does is call all of his friends and say, "This is what we're buying. Do you have anything you want to bring me?" We had a friend over for dinner who started talking about the kind of show he wanted to pitch to someone he used to work with and my husband said, "I control a comic book like that." Within a week, they were having the meeting and sold the show.

I have several women friends who are entertainment industry executives. Not one of them has ever done anything like that for me. One got a new job at a company where a script of mine would be a perfect fit, so I called her and asked to submit it. She flat out said that she couldn't start bringing friends' scripts in right away, but I should call her in a year – *a year* – because then she'd have a few successes under her belt and could consider it. It never occurred to her that buying from her friends could be the fastest, easiest way to score a few wins.

Being female, and thus thinking this lack of network assistance might be my fault, I started asking around to see what was the norm for us. Sure enough, in my survey, no female writer or producer had ever gotten a call like that from another woman, no female executive I asked had ever made a call like that, and all of the men I spoke with thought that we were doing it the same way they did, which is to hire the friends who they know will do a good job and won't make them look bad. They actually didn't believe we weren't doing that. Maybe that explains why only seven percent of all studio films are written or directed by women. The men take care of their own and assume we're doing the same.

Once again, this is the problem of being a Retriever in an industry controlled by Shepherds. The few Retrievers who make it into the inner circle are terrified that if they start calling all the Retrievers they know and hiring them, someone will notice, and they'll lose the place they fought so hard for.

They're also worried that if they hire a Retriever who does a bad job, they'll be blamed, despite the fact that Shepherds hire each other and screw things up all the time, and rarely does it come back to haunt them. Maybe because they don't go around apologizing to everyone for hiring another Shepherd, and the Shepherds they hire don't spend all day thanking them. It's just business as usual for Shepherds to hire other Shepherds.

Women also don't help each other out nearly to the extent we should once on the job. Again, we want to be seen as able to hang with the Shepherds, and when we see a Retriever struggling, our first reaction is to distance ourselves from her, lest we be seen in the same light.

Often when someone has a legitimate complaint that she would be treated differently if she were a man, the entire workforce can point to a woman who is treating her that way, as if that in any way negates the point.

Women treat other women in the workplace with less respect than they treat men, and it is despicable. Try to be very aware of when you are doing this and stop it.

And if you ever are in a position to hire, recruit, contract with, buy products from, book for speaking, bring on as a consultant or refer business to one of your qualified friends, who just happens to be a woman, DO IT! That's what men do.

## 5. Don't Tell Yourself You're Not Worthy!

Both practicing law and working as an investment banker, I would often sit at my desk and wonder when someone was going to come in and call me out for being a total fraud. When would they figure out that I didn't belong there at all? My mother tells me she used to have that same feeling as an insurance adjuster. My sister has it now and then, despite being a top headhunter, one of the best in her market.

I occasionally have it as a public speaker, even though I always get a hugely positive response after a talk or workshop. No one has ever asked for their money back, and yet, when someone calls to book me, and we start discussing rates, a voice in the back of my head will start saying, "Hope they don't figure out you're not worth all this money."

Recently, the Directors Guild of America honored Mimi Leder as a Pioneering Director. Her daughter, Hannah, made a beautiful speech about her mother that included this statement: "The day before any movie or show starts, my mom spends the day walking around the house saying, 'I'm a fraud. What if they find out I don't know what I'm doing? What if they show up on set and make me stop because I don't belong there?'"

Mimi Leder feels this way! The Emmy-award winning Director of *ER*. Steven Spielberg's hand-picked choice to direct Dreamworks' first feature film, *The Peacemaker*, and then, because that was so successful, the studio's second film, *Deep Impact*. Her credits are extensive and impressive, and she is one of my personal heroes in this industry, and yet, *she* still wonders when she's going to be "found out."

I asked Mimi if I could include that story in this book and she instantly said, "Yes." She knows how critical it is for women to help other women, even if it means sharing something as personal and private as the fear of being called a fraud, despite being one of the most accomplished professionals in your industry. We have to start talking about these things, and we have to be aware that we aren't the only ones feeling this way.

Every woman I have ever spoken to who works in a competitive field knows this feeling. Most men don't. Why do we do this to ourselves?

Don't tell yourself you don't belong.
Don't question your own worth.
Don't call yourself a fraud.

You're not!

# 6. Don't Denigrate Other Women!!

Worse than not lifting other women up, as discussed above, is tearing other women down. There is nothing more disagreeable than an office gossip, who is almost always a woman, and is almost always talking about other women, and not kindly.

Also, be very judicious about what you're willing to say or believe about the women in your workplace.

A former housemate of mine was an assistant to the head of a film production company for several years when she finally got promoted to Creative Executive, which meant she was now responsible for finding and developing material that could be made into movies.

She found a book she thought would make a great film, her boss agreed, and she became the point person for the whole project, reading samples from potential writers, helping to choose who to hire, reading all of their drafts, finding a Director, getting the movie greenlit and choosing locations.

They decided to film in Louisiana, so she began working with the Film Commission there to put together a locations package. With several location options for each scene, it was time for her boss and the Director to go scout them. Then, to her surprise, her boss told her she was going. In fact, he was a bit stunned that she didn't realize all along that she'd be going, since this movie was her project and she knew more about where they were visiting than either of the men.

The trip came and it was a huge success – her first business trip ever and she was ecstatic. Then, the following week, when she was back in the office, a woman she worked with made an off-color comment about her relationship with her boss, intimating that it was something other than professional.

My housemate was stunned, and when she pressed her to explain what she was talking about, the woman – a friend of hers, or so she thought – said, "Well, he took you to Louisiana instead of his wife."

Think about that. My housemate had worked long and hard to earn the right to go on that trip, and while on it continued to prove her worth to the company, and all the small-minded bitches back in the office could think was that she and her boss were having an affair. How can any woman advance if the ignorance and petty jealousy of other women causes them to start those kinds of rumors?

I have seen this dynamic play out over and over. A woman I went to Berkeley Law with was a beautiful young blonde, a wife and mother, who happened to be fluent in Chinese. So when a partner in her firm was going on a trip to China, he asked her to join him. It was all proceeding perfectly until his *wife* refused to let her go. That's right – his wife had a problem with the young blonde attorney traveling with her husband, and he capitulated and excluded her from the trip.

That is so limiting to a woman's career, and it is generally at the hands of other women. When I was practicing law, my deal team partner was the most honorable, respectable lawyer I've ever known, and I learned so much from him, principally because those kinds of rumors never plagued our relationship. We had one year in which he had dinner with me more often than he had dinner with his wife, and one month in that year when he spent the night with me more often than with his wife, working either in the office or on the road.

Fifteen years after my deal team partner and I both left the firm, my husband and I went to his and his wife's

25th wedding anniversary party, and I took her aside and thanked her for my extraordinary career. She knew right away what I meant, and she said, "What else was I going to do? Stop him from working with the person he needed?"

When he and I worked those insane hours, I was 26 years old and I had paid for law school, in part, by working as a runway model. There's a lot she could have done to stop us from working together, but she didn't. For that, I will be forever grateful to both of them – him for being a mentor and her for being a secure enough person to allow another woman to thrive in her career.

Given all of the above, the next point goes without saying, but I'll say it anyway...

# 7. Don't Have Sex With Your Boss!!!

This is the most critical thing I can tell you, as a woman, trying to have a career in any business. It is the most damaging thing you can do to yourself, and the most damaging thing you can do to other women in your industry. It's the reason women start rumors about other women, because sometimes they're true.

If you and your boss are both single, and you strike up a relationship and it progresses towards something real and permanent, you may be able to manage staying together while advancing in your career, but you must realize that your advancement may be forever tainted.

On the other hand, if your boss is married, this will not go well for you. Having an affair with a married superior generally goes far worse for the woman than it does for the man. It is always damaging to her career and future prospects, and it will follow her forever, particularly in the information age, where no secret is safe.

Let me reiterate: **an affair always harms the woman in the workplace**.

Do not think you are the exception to this rule! If you are even close to tempted to have sex with your boss, imagine the very different life the young Monica Lewinsky could have had if her boss, a married man nearly twice her age, had known better. Remember the attacks on the actress, Kristen Stewart, a girl who grew up on film sets, being told how important and powerful the Director is? She was vilified for having sex with Rupert Sanders, even though she was far younger and not the one committing adultery.

Even now, you may be thinking, "Those girls knew what they were doing."

In response, please consider the facts of those two affairs: the most powerful man at a workplace, married, in his mid 40s, starts a sexual relationship with the 21 or 22 year-old girl who works for him 12-15 hours a day. This describes both Kristen Stewart and Monica Lewinsky's affairs. Do you still feel they were the culpable ones? And yet they shouldered the majority of the blame, and the fallout.

No good comes for the woman from getting involved with her married boss. You may be able to come up with one or two exceptions that you've seen in real life, but the great majority of these relationships leave a swath of destruction in her world while his remains virtually unscathed.

Don't do it.

# FINAL THOUGHTS

One of the reasons women don't advance in male-designed workplaces is that we check out before reaching the brass ring. Some would call this giving up, or failing, but I see it as simply choosing a path with greater personal rewards, which is a form of success, too.

No woman has any obligation to keep swimming against the current. It's exhausting and can have limited returns, and it causes us to blame ourselves for our lack of advancement, which is not always the case.

But it's also not always that we're being held down by external forces. Often we simply have to learn to work against our own instincts and develop traits that will catapult us to the next level.

If you want to succeed, advance and be rewarded in your chosen field, and that field follows the hunter/warrior paradigm of rewarding aggression, competition and quick decision-making, then you have to start swimming with that current. You have to make it easier to get to your goals, which you can do by recognizing the areas where your natural instincts don't match the requirements of your workplace, and then, adapt.

The system is designed so that the highest rewards go to the people who designed the system, and the system isn't changing, at least not radically or anytime soon.

The only way to reach that peak is to do what it takes to be rewarded and recognized within the system in which you want to work. Those few Retrievers who are in the upper ranks got there by out-herding the Shepherds. It wasn't easy, but they did it. You can, too.

To succeed in male-designed workplaces, women are the ones who need to adapt.

For now.

# THE TALK

This book was inspired by the talk, "How Women Can Succeed in the Workplace (Despite Having "Female Brains") by Valerie Alexander, and includes examples from various presentations that have been customized for specific industries: entertainment, law, finance, or a general audience of female professionals, undergraduates or graduate students.

The talk can be delivered as a keynote or workshop, and includes slides and video not contained here.

To bring Valerie to your campus, company, conference or organization to deliver this informative, entertaining talk to your audience, employees, class or members, please reach out to info@SpeakHappiness.com.

Valerie also offers the inspirational "Speak Happiness!" series of workshops and keynotes, helping companies, employees, entrepreneurs, artists and others stay positive, move forward, increase productivity and maximize profits by making happiness a priority.

If you'd like to get on the Speak Happiness mailing list and receive two free Happiness workbooks, please sign up at http://www.speakhappiness.com/hello/.

For a free chapter of Valerie Alexander's next book, *Success as a Second Language: A Guidebook for Defining and Achieving Personal Success*, and to join the Successful Female Brains mailing list, please go to http://www.speakhappiness.com/success-for-you/

# ABOUT THE AUTHOR

Valerie Alexander is the author of "Happiness as a Second Language: A Guidebook to Achieving Lasting, Permanent Happiness," and is the creator of the "... as a Second Language" series of self-help guides.

As a screenwriter, Valerie has worked with Joel Schumacher, Catherine Zeta Jones, Barry Sonnenfeld, Ice Cube and others. She co-wrote, produced and directed the award-winning short film, "Making the Cut," as well as numerous commercials and public service announcements.

As a professional speaker, Valerie travels the country with her entertaining and informative talks, "How Women Can Succeed in the Workplace (Despite Having Female Brains)" and her inspirational "Speak Happiness!" series of workshops and keynotes, helping companies, employees, entrepreneurs, artists and others stay positive, move forward, increase productivity and maximize profits by making happiness a priority. For more details about all of her talks, please visit her Speaker Page.

Valerie spent her early career in the Silicon Valley where she worked on some of the most significant transactions of the Internet era as a securities lawyer, a venture capital consultant, an investment banker and an Internet executive.

Valerie received her B.A. from Trinity University and her J.D. and M.S. degrees from the University of California, Berkeley. In the spring of 2010, she was invited back to Berkeley Law to teach the legal ethics seminar, "Representation of Law in Film."

She currently lives in Los Angeles with her husband, writer-producer Rick Alexander, and their ill-mannered German Shepherd, Pepper.

## Other Books by Valerie Alexander

*Happiness as a Second Language*

*Success as a Second Language*